colorcats

ALSO BY MARGARET GATES ROOT:

Color Cats Book One
Color Cats Book Two - Kitty Tales

COLOR CATS

KITTY SKETCH

COLORING NOTEBOOK

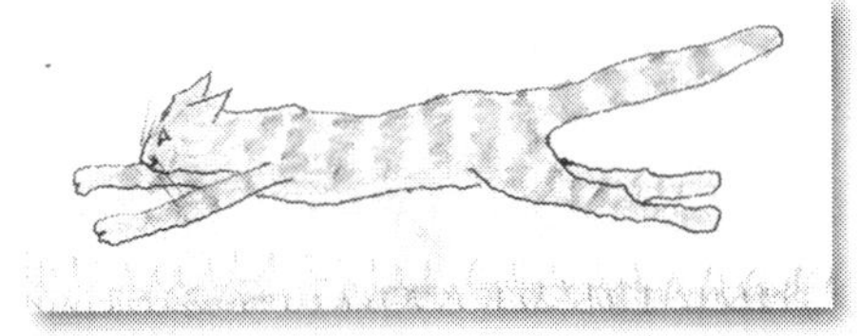

MARGARET GATES ROOT

Clowder Books

ISBN 978-0-9968995-2-9

Printed in the United States of America

colorcats.org

For my husband, Ashley.

A note from the author:

Whenever I leave a note for my husband, I add a quick little sketch to dress it up. A whimsical drawing of one of our numerous cats or the ubiquitous backyard squirrels. He looks forward to the little images so much that I started leaving a new drawing every day, minus the note.

I am sharing some of my favorites with you, in black and white, so you can add your own color. I hope you enjoy them, too.

Margaret

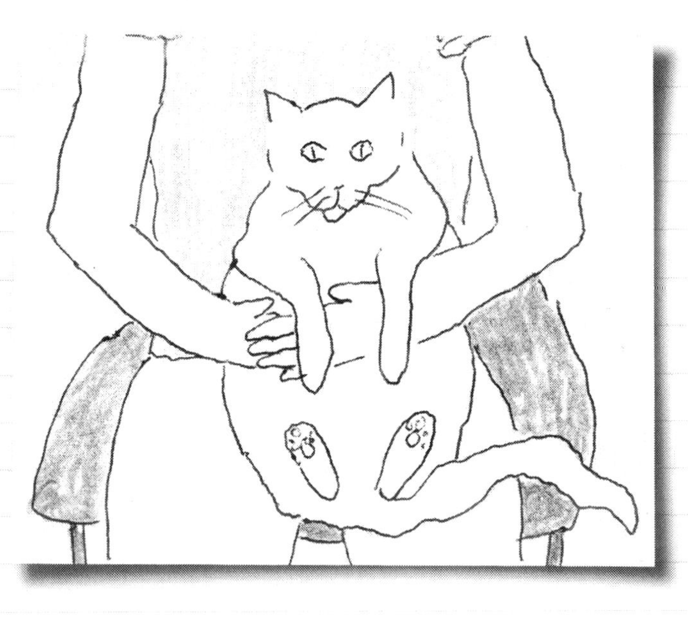

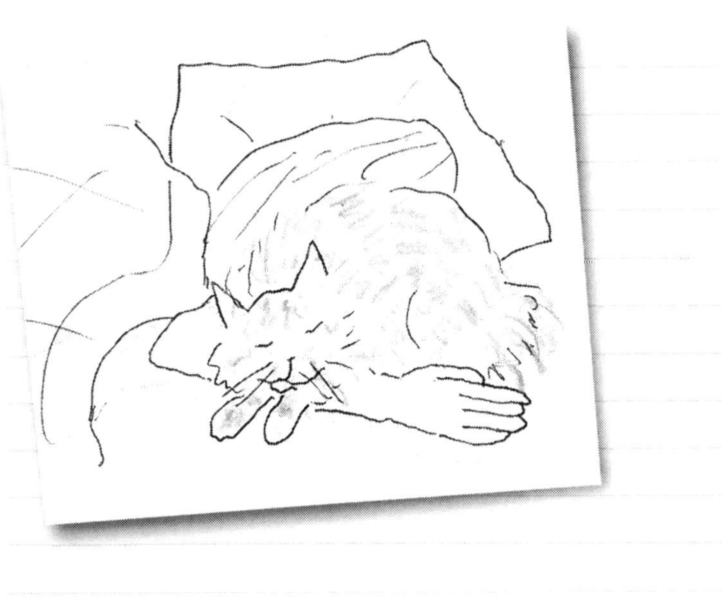

HAPPY
BIRTHDAY!

CATNIP

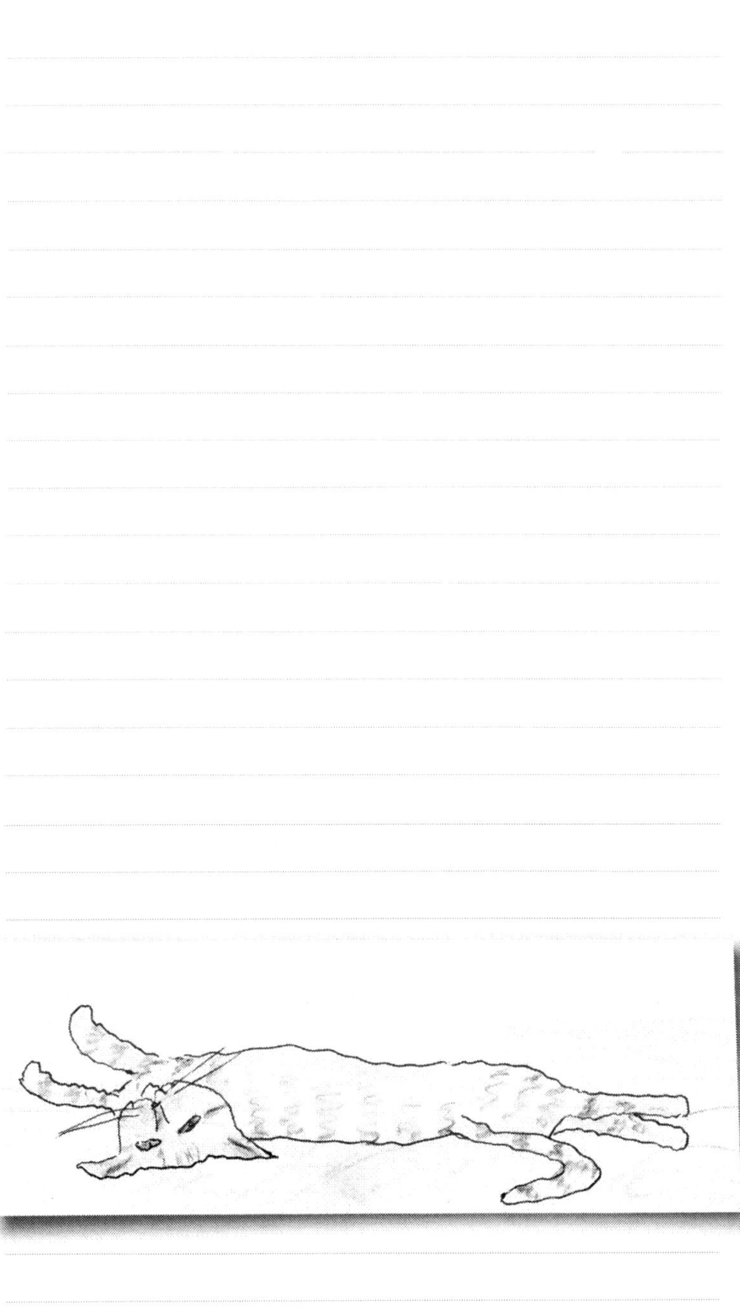

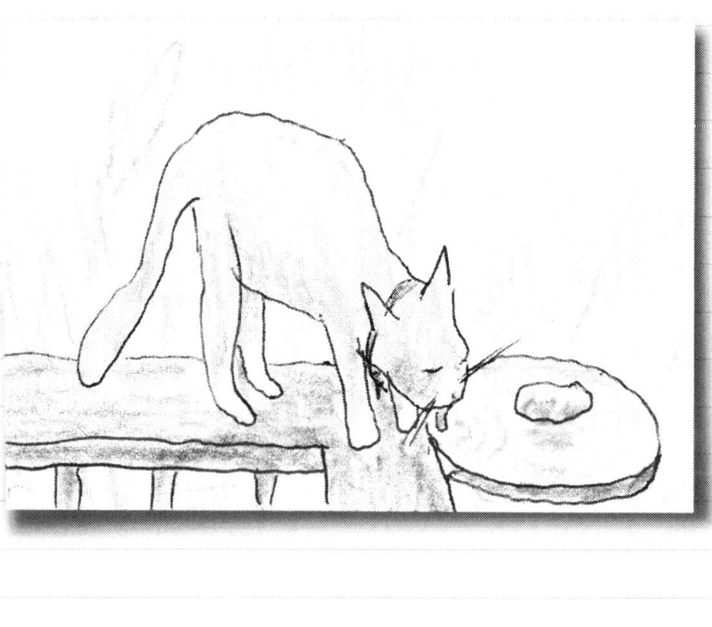

Margaret Gates Root is the founder of the Feline Nutrition Foundation, a non-profit organization dedicated to helping our feline companions lead healthier, happier lives by educating pet parents on the benefits of bio-appropriate nutrition for cats.

For more information, visit the Foundation at
FelineNutritionFoundation.org

If you enjoyed this book, please consider reviewing it on the purchase site. Reviews help books be more visible to customers. Besides, I want to know what you liked about it.

Made in the USA
Charleston, SC
03 November 2016